AN

AA'S
LITTLE HANDBOOK OF

HOPE
PRAYERS
INSPIRATION
& LAUGHS

LEAVE AN AMAZON
PRODUCT REVIEW
Available in five countries

VISIT THE BOLD & BRAVE
www.addictionrecoverybooks.com

VISIT IMAGINATE PUBLISHING
www.imaginateonline.com

An

AA's

Little Handbook Of

HOPE
PRAYERS
INSPIRATION
& LAUGHS

Includes AA Acronyms, AA Prayers
Jokes, & Little Quotes From Big Names
for Recovering Alcoholics and Other Addicts

An AA's Little Handbook Of Hope Prayers Inspiration &
Laughs by DIANA LEA

First Printing, 2022
First Edition 2022
ISBN- 9798441303309

Disclaimer: Every reasonable effort has been made to
ensure the information in this book was correct at the time
of publication. The author and publisher do not assume and
hereby disclaim any responsibility and/or liability for any
loss, damage, disruption, or adverse effects resulting from
the use of the information found within this book, whether
by errors, omissions, negligence, accident, or any other
cause.

Books published by Imaginate Publishing are available at
special discount rates for bulk purchases by corporations,
institutions, and other organizations. For more
information, please contact Imaginate Publishing at
info@imaginateonline.com

Contents Herein

I have held many things in my hands and have lost them all; but what I put in God's hands; I still have.

My Thoughts & Stuff

Although we may have taken all 12 Steps, we are not finished walking them. We may be forever finding ourselves stepping back. We are human. We faulter. We tend to fall into the trap of our old ways. But we remind ourselves, or be reminded by our peers, of the prison we came from and the freedom we have found.

Keep this little book handy at all times lest you ever forget where you came from, where you're going, and why.

Oh, and if you don't have a Higher Power, I'll let you borrow mine. 😊

The 12 Promises (p 83)

1. If we are painstaking about this phase of our development, we will be amazed before we are halfway through.
2. We are going to know a new freedom and a new happiness.
3. We will not regret the past nor wish to shut the door on it.
4. We will comprehend the word serenity and we will know peace.
5. No matter how far down the scale we have gone, we will see how our experience can benefit others.
6. That feeling of uselessness and self-pity will disappear.
7. We will lose interest in selfish things and gain interest in our fellows.
8. Self-seeking will slip away.
9. Our whole attitude and outlook upon life will change.
10. Fear of people and of economic insecurity will leave us.
11. We will intuitively know how to handle situations which used to baffle us.
12. We will suddenly realize that God is doing for us what we could not do for ourselves.

Footprints in the Sand

One night I dreamed a dream.

As I was walking along the beach with my God. Across the dark sky flashed scenes from my life. For each scene, I noticed two sets of footprints in the sand, One belonging to me and one to my God.

After the last scene of my life flashed before me, I looked back at the footprints in the sand. I noticed that at many times along the path of my life, especially at the very lowest and saddest times, there was only one set of footprints. This really troubled me, so I asked the Lord about it.

"God, you said once I decided to follow you, you'd walk with me all the way. But I noticed that during the saddest and most troublesome times of my life, there was only one set of footprints. I don't understand why, when I needed You the most, You would leave me."

He whispered, "My precious child, I love you and will never leave you. Never, ever, during your trials and testing's. When you saw only one set of footprints, It was then that I carried you."

Step Twelve Love Poem

The wonderful love of a beautiful maid,
And the love of a staunch true man,
And the love of a baby that's unafraid -
All have existed since time began.
But the most wonderful love,
The Love of all loves,
Even greater than the love for Mother,
Is the infinite, tenderest, passionate love,
Of one drunken bum for another.

The Alcoholic's Prayer

In the past several hours (so far today), I have not hurt anyone. I have not had a drink. I haven't lost my temper, haven't gossiped, haven't been greedy, nasty, grumpy, or self-centered. For that I am grateful. But in few minutes, I'm going to get out of bed, and then I'm going to need a lot of help.

Prayers When You Need Them

Serenity Prayer: The original form of the prayer is attributed to the theologian Reinhold Niebuhr...

God grant me the serenity
To accept the things I cannot change;
Courage to change the things I can;
And wisdom to know the difference.
Living one day at a time;
Enjoying one moment at a time;
Accepting hardships as the pathway to peace;
Taking, as He did, this sinful world
As it is, not as I would have it;
Trusting that He will make things right
If I surrender to His Will;
So that I may be reasonably happy in this life
And supremely happy with Him
Forever and ever in the next.

The Set Aside Prayer:

Please help me to set aside everything I think I know about [*people, place, or thing*] so I may have an open mind and a new experience. Please help me to see the truth about [*people, place or thing*]. (From, "To the Agnostic".)

First Step Prayer

Help me to see and admit that I am powerless over my alcoholism. Help me to understand how my alcoholism has led to unmanageability in my life. Help me this day to understand the true meaning of powerlessness. Remove from me all denial of my alcoholism. (From, "More About Alcoholism".)

Second Step Prayer

I am having trouble with personal relationships. I can't control my emotional nature. I am prey to misery and depression. I can't make a living. I feel useless. I am full of fear. I am unhappy. I can't seem to be of real help to others. I know in my heart that only you can restore me to sanity if I am just willing to stop doubting your power. I humbly ask that you help me to understand that it is more powerful to believe than not to believe and that you are either everything or nothing. (p. 52:2, 52:3, 53:1, 53:2)

Third Step Prayer

I offer myself to You — to build with me and to do with me as You will. Relieve me of the bondage of self, that I may better do Your will. Take away my difficulties, that victory over them may bear witness to those I would help of Your Power, Your Love, and Your Way of life. May I do Your will always! (63:2 original manuscript)

A Pre-Inventory Fourth Step Prayer:

Please help me to honestly take stock. Help me to search out the flaws in my make-up which caused my failure. Help me to see where resentment has plagued me and resulted in spiritual malady, but more importantly help me to understand my part in these resentments. Help me to resolutely look for my own mistakes and to understand where I had been selfish, dishonest, self-seeking and frightened. Please help me to be searching and fearless in my endeavor to write my inventory. (p. 64:2, 64:3, 67:2)

Fourth Step Prayer (Resentments)

When a person offends me, help me to remember this is a sick person. Help me to show the same tolerance, pity, and patience that I would cheerfully grant a sick friend. This is a sick person. Show me how can I be helpful to this person. Save me from being angry. Your will be done. (p. 67)

A Fourth Step Resentment Prayer:

Please help me to be free of anger and see that the world and its people have dominated me. Show me that the wrong-doing of others, fancied or real, has the power to actually kill me. Help me to master my resentments by understanding that the people who wrong me were perhaps sick too. Please help me show those I resent the same tolerance, pity and patience that I would cheerfully grant a sick friend. Help me to see that this is a sick man. Please show me how I can be helpful to him and save me from being angry. Help me avoid retaliation or argument. I know I can't be helpful to all people, but at least show me how to take a kindly and tolerant view of each and every one. Thy will be done."(66:2, 66:3, 66:4, 67:0, 67:1)

Fourth Step Freedom from Bondage Prayer
I have a resentment towards a person that I want to be free of. So, I am asking you to give this person everything I want for myself. Help me to feel compassionate understanding and love for this person. I pray that they will receive everything they need. Thank you for your help and strength with this resentment. (p. 552)

Fourth Step Sex Inventory Prayer:
Help me review my own conduct over the years past. Show me where I have been selfish, dishonest, or inconsiderate. Show me whom I have hurt and where I have unjustifiably aroused jealousy, suspicion or bitterness. Help me to see where I was at fault and what I should have done instead. Help me to be fearless and searching in my endeavor to write my sexual inventory. (69:1)

Fourth Step Sex Prayer:

Please grace me with guidance in each questionable situation, sanity, and strength to do the right thing. If sex becomes very troublesome, quiet my imperious urge, help me not to yield and keep me from heartache as I throw myself the harder into helping others. Help me think of their needs and help me work for them. (69:2, 69:3, 70:2)

Fourth Step Sex Inventory Prayer:

Please help me to be free of fear as I attempt to shine the spotlight of truth across my past sex relations. Please show me where my behavior has harmed others and help me to see the truth these relationships hold for me. Help me see where I have been at fault and what I should have done differently. (p. 69)

Fourth Step Sex Prayer:

Please help me mold my sex ideals and help me to live up to them. Help me be willing to grow toward my ideals and help me be willing to make amends where I have done harm. Please show me what to do in each specific matter, and be the final judge in each situation. Help me avoid hysterical thinking or advice. (69:2, 69:3)

Fourth Step Sanity and Strength Prayer

I earnestly pray for the right ideal, for guidance in each questionable situation, for sanity, and for the strength to do the right thing. (p. 70)

Fourth Step Fear Prayer:

Thank you for helping me be honest enough to see this truth about myself and now that you have shown me the truth about my fears, please remove these fears from me. Please help me outgrow my fears and direct my attention to what you would have me be. Demonstrate through me and help me become that which you would have me be. Help me do Your will always. (68:3)

Fourth Step Fear Prayer

I ask that you remove my fear and direct my attention to what you would have me be. (p. 68)

A Pre-Fifth Step Prayer:

Please help me to complete my housecleaning by admitting to another human being the exact nature of my wrongs. Please remove any fears I have about this step and show me how completion of it will remove my egotism and fear. Help me to see how this step builds my character through humility, fearlessness and honesty. Direct me to the right person who will keep my confidence and fully understand and approve what I am driving at. Then help me to pocket my pride and go to it, illuminating every twist of character, every dark cranny of the past so I may complete this step and begin to feel near to you. (72:1, 72:2, 73:0, 74:2, 75:2)

Fifth Step Prayer

Thank you for helping me complete my house-cleaning. I can now look the world in the eye. I can be alone at perfect peace and ease. My fears have fallen from me. I have begun to feel your nearness. I have begun to have a spiritual experience. I feel I am on the Broad Highway, walking hand in hand with the Spirit of the Universe. (75:2)

Fifth Step Quiet Hour Prayer:

Thank You for giving me the strength, faith and courage I needed to get through my 5th Step. I thank you from the bottom of my heart for helping me to know you better, by showing me what has been blocking me from you. Please show me if I have omitted anything and help me to honestly see if my stones are properly in place or if I have skimped in any area of this work. (75:3)

Sixth Step prayer:

Thank you for removing my fear and for showing me the truth about myself. I need your help to become willing to let go of the things in me which continue to block me off from you. Please grant me your grace and make me willing to have these objectionable characteristics, defects and short-comings removed. (76:1)

Sixth Step Prayer

I am ready for Your help in removing from me the defects of character which I now realize are an obstacle to my recovery. Help me to continue being honest with myself & guide me toward spiritual & mental health. (76:1)

Seventh Step Prayer

I am now willing that you should have all of me, good & bad. I pray that you now remove from me every single defect of character which stands in the way of my usefulness to you & my fellows. Grant me strength, as I go out from here to do Your bidding." (76:2)

Eighth Step Prayer:

Please remove my Fears and show me your truth. Show me all the harms I have caused with my behavior and help me be willing to make amends to one and all. Help me to be willing to go to any lengths for victory over alcohol. (76:3)

Nineth Step Prayer:

With regard to this amend, give me the strength, courage and direction to do the right thing, no matter what the personal consequences may be. Help me not to shrink from anything. Help me not to delay if it can be avoided. Help me to be sensible, tactful, considerate and humble without being servile or scraping. (79:1, 83:3)

Nineth Step prayer for the Spouse:

Please show me how to make amends to my Spouse. Help me to keep my Spouse's happiness Uppermost in my mind as I try, with your Grace, to make this relationship right. (82:1)

Nineth Step Prayer for the Family:

Please show me how to find the way of Patience, Tolerance, Kindness and Love in my heart, my Mind and my Soul. Show me how to demonstrate these principles to my family and all those about me. (83:1)

Nineth Step Prayer:

I pray that I may be given strength and direction to do the right thing, no matter what the personal consequences may be. (79)

Tenth Step Nightly Review Prayer:

Help me to constructively review my day. Where was I resentful, selfish, dishonest or afraid? Do I owe an apology? Have I kept something to myself which should be discussed with another person at once? Was I kind and loving toward all? What could I have done better? Was I thinking of myself most of the time? Or was I thinking of what I could do for others, of what I could pack into the stream of life? Please forgive me for my harms and wrongs today and let me know corrective measures I should be take. (86:2)

Tenth Step Amends Prayer:

Please forgive me for my failings today. I know that because of my failings, I was not able to be as effective as I could have been for you. Please forgive me and help me live Your will better today. I ask you now to show me how to correct the errors I have just outlined. Guide me and direct me. Please remove my arrogance and my fear. Show me how to make my relationships right and grant me the humility and strength to do Your will. (86:1)

Tenth Step Prayer:

Please help me review my day. Please grant me the willingness to see what you would have me see, in the light you would have me see it: free from morbid reflection, fear, obsessive guilt, and dishonesty.

Tenth Step Prayer:

My prayer is to best serve you. I pray I may continue to grow in understanding & effectiveness. Help me to watch for selfishness, dishonesty, resentment and fear. Help me to be willing to have You remove them at once. I must be willing to discuss them with someone immediately. I will make amends quickly if I have harmed anyone. And then I will turn my thoughts toward helping someone else. Please help me to remember to practice love and tolerance of others. (84:2)

Tenth Step Nightly Prayer

Forgive me where I have been resentful, selfish, dishonest or afraid today. Help me to not keep any-thing to myself but to discuss it all openly with another person. Show me where I owe an apology and help me make it. Help me to be kind and loving to all people. Show me how I could have done better today. Use me in the mainstream of life. Free me of worry, remorse, or morbid reflections that I may be of usefulness to others.

An Eleventh Step Prayer:
(Prayer of St. Francis, actually from the early 1900s)
Lord, make me an instrument of thy peace.
Where there is hatred, let me sow love;
Where there is injury, pardon;
Where there is doubt, faith;
Where there is despair, hope;
Where there is darkness, light;
Where there is sadness, joy.

O divine Master, grant that I may not so much seek
To be consoled as to console,
To be understood as to understand,
To be loved as to love;
For it is in giving that we receive;
It is in pardoning that we are pardoned;
It is in dying to self that we are born to eternal life.

11th Step Prayer for Growth and Effectiveness:
Please help me Watch for Selfishness, Dishonesty,
Resentment and Fear. When these crop up in me,
help me to immediately ask you to remove them
from me and help me discuss these feelings with
someone. Help me to quickly make amends if I
have harmed anyone and help me to resolutely turn
my thoughts to someone I can Help. Help me to be
Loving and Tolerant of everyone today. 84:2)

Eleventh Step Morning Prayer:
Should I find myself agitated, doubtful or indecisive today, please give me inspiration, help me to have an intuitive thought or a decision about this problem I face. Help me not to struggle, instead, help me to relax and take it easy. Help me know what I should do and keep me mindful, that you are running the show. Free me from my bondage of self. Your will be done always. (86:3)

Eleventh Step A Prayer:
Please direct my thinking and keep my thoughts divorced from self – pity, dishonest or self-seeking motives. Please keep my thought life clear from wrong motives and help me employ my mental faculties, that my thought-life might be placed on a higher plane, the plane of inspiration." (86:2)

Eleventh Step Morning Prayer:
Please show me all through this day, what my next step is to be and please grace me with whatever I need to take care of the problems in my life today. I ask especially that you free me from the bondage of self-will."(87:1)

Eleventh Step Morning Prayer
Show me the way of patience, tolerance, kindness and love. (p. 83)

Eleventh Step During the Day Prayer

I am agitated (doubtful). Please give me the right thought or action. I am no longer running the show. Your will be done. (p. 87)

Twelfth Step Prayer

Having had a spiritual experience, I must now remember that "faith without works is dead." And practical experience shows that nothing will so much insure immunity from drinking as intensive work with other alcoholics. So, please help me to carry this message to other alcoholics! Provide me with the guidance and wisdom to talk with another alcoholic because I can help when no one else can. Help me secure his confidence and remember he is ill. (89:1)

My Own Prayers:

My Own Prayers:

My Own Prayers:

My Own Prayers:

My Own Prayers:

My Own Prayers:

_____
_____
_____
_____
_____
_____
_____
_____
_____
_____
_____
_____
_____
_____
_____
_____
_____
_____
_____
_____
_____

An AA's Acronym Guide

I thought it would be appropriate to begin with the acronym for SERENITY, since we use it so much, then move on alphabetically from there.

SERENITY

See things for what they are

Everything happens for a reason

Rely on God for the answer

Engage in prayer when you are in need

Never give up on God because God never gives up on you

Illustrate character by example

Try forgiveness

Yesterday learn from, today learn towards, tomorrow learn to

*****

AA

Absolute Abstinence
Altered Attitudes
Altruistic Action
Attitude Adjustment
*****

AA's-R-US

Alcoholics Anonymous Recovery Unity Service
*****

ABC

Acceptance, Belief, Change
*****

ACTION

Any Change Toward Improving One's Nature
Any Change To Improve Our Natures
*****

ADDICT

Anybody Doing Drugs In Compulsive Trouble
*****

AFGE

Another Fucking Growth Experience
*****

AIDS

Active In Dangerous Sex
 Addicts Injecting Dirty Syringes
     *****

ALCOHOLICS

A Life Centered On Helping Others Live In
Complete Sobriety
     *****

ANONYMOUS

Actions Not Our Names Yield Maintenance Of
Unity & Service
     *****

ANGER

A No-Good Energy Rising
     *****

ASK

Ass-Saving Kit
     *****

BAR

Beware, Alcohol, Run
Beware Alcohol Ruin
     *****

BIG BOOK

Believing In God Beats Our Old Knowledge

*****

BS

Before Sobriety

*****

BUT

Being Unconvinced Totally

*****

CALM

Can Anger Leave Me

*****

CARE

Comforting And Reassuring Each Other…

*****

CHANGE

Choosing Honesty Allows New Growth Every-day

*****

CIA

Catholic Irish Alcoholic

*****

CLEAN

Completely Leaving Every Addiction Now!

*****

COURAGE

'Cause Of Using Recovery's A Great Effort

*****

CRAP

Carry Resentments Against People

*****

DAMM

Drunks Against Mad Mothers

*****

DEAD

Drinking Ends All Dreams

*****

DENIAL

Don't Even Notice I Am Lying
Don't Even Notice It's A Lie

*****

DETACH

Don't Even Think About Changing Him/Her

*****

DT'S

Don't Think Shit
*****

DUES

Desperately Using Everything But Sobriety
*****

EDI not DIE

Easy Does It not Does It Easy
*****

EGO

Easing God Out
Edging God Out
*****

FAILURE

Fearful, Arrogant, Insecure, Lonely, Uncertain, Resentful, Empty
*****

FAITH

Fear Ain't In This House
Facing An Inner Truth Heals
For An Instant Trust Him
Fantastic Adventure In Trusting Him

FAITH

Fear And Insecurity? Trust Him!

*****

FAMILY

Father And Mother I Love You
Forget About Me I Love You

*****

FEAR

Failure Expected And Received
False Evidence Appearing Real
Feelings Expressed Allows Relief
Feelings Every Alcoholic Rejects
Fighting Ego Against Reality
Forget Everything And Run
Fuck Everything And Run
Face Everything And Recover!
Forgetting Everything's All Right
Frantic Effort to Appear Real
Frantic Efforts to Appear Recovered
Fight Everyone And Relapse

*****

FINE

Faithful, Involved, Knowledgeable, Experienced
Feeling Insecure, Numb and Empty

FINE

Frantic, Insane, Nuts and Egotistical
Freaked out, Insecure, Neurotic and Emotional
Feeling Insecure Neurotic & Emotional
Frustrated, Insecure, Neurotic & Emotional
Fucked, Insecure, Neurotic & Emotional
Fucked up, Insecure, Neurotic, & Emotional
*****

FOG

Fear of God
*****

FUCKED

Feeling Useless 'Cause I'm Kicking Every Drug
*****

GAYS

Go Ask Your Sponsor
*****

GIFT

God Is Forever There
*****

GIFTS

Getting It From The Steps
*****

GOD

Good Orderly Direction
Get Out Devil
Go On Dreaming
Group Of Drunks
*****

GOYA

Get Off Your Ass
*****

GUT

God's Undeniable Truths
*****

HALT

Honestly, Actively, Lovingly Tolerant
Hope, Acceptance, Love & Tolerance
*****

HALTS FEAR

Hope, Acceptance, Love & Tolerance Stops
Forgetting That Everything's All Right
*****

HEART

Healing Enjoying and Recovering Together
*****

HELP

His Ever-Loving Presence
Her Ever-Loving Presence
Hope, Encouragement, Love and Patience
*****

HIT

Hang In There
*****

HOPE

Happy Our Program Exists
Hearing Other Peoples' Experience
Hang On! Peace Exists
Hold On Pain Ends
*****

HOW

Honesty, Open-Mindedness, Willingness
Honest, Open-Minded and Willing
*****

ISM

I, Self, Me
I See Me
Incredibly Short Memory
In Side Me
I Sabotage Myself

ISM

I Sponsor Myself
Internal Spiritual Malady
　*****

KISS

Keep It Simple, Stupid
Keep It Simple, Sugar
Keep It Simple, Sweetheart
Keeping It Simple, Spiritually
　*****

LET GO

Leave Everything To God, Okay?
　*****

LOVE

Living Our Victories Everyday
　*****

MMM

Meetings, Meditation & Masturbation (for the first year)
　*****

NEW

Nothing Else Worked
*****

NOW

No Other Way
*****

NOWHERE or NOWHERE
*****

NUTS

Not Using The Steps
*****

OUR

Openly Using Recovery
*****

PACE

Positive Attitudes Change Everything
*****

PAID

Pitiful And Incomprehensible Demoralization
*****

PAIN

Pause And Invite New
*****

PHD

Pretty Heavy Drinker
*****

PMS

Pour More Scotch
Pour Me Syndrome
*****

PRIDE

Personal Recovery Involves Defeating Ego
*****

PROGRAM

People Relying On God Relaying A Message
*****

PUSH

Pray Until Something Happens
*****

Q-TIP

Quit Taking It Personally *****

RAGE

Real Angry Gut-level Ego
*****

RELAPSE

Recovery Exits Life And Program Seem Empty.
*****

RELATIONSHIP

Really Exciting Love Affair Turns Into Outrageous
Nightmare Sobriety Hangs In Peril
*****

RID

Restless, Irritable and Discontented
*****

SASTO

Some Are Sicker Than Others
*****

SHIT

Simply How I'm Thinking…
*****

SLIP

Sobriety Loses Its Priority *****

SOB

Sober Old Bastard
Sober Old Biker
Sober Old Bitch

SOB

Sober Old Bag

*****

SOBER

Staying Off Booze Enjoying Recovery
Son Of A Bitch, Everything's Real

*****

SOBRIETY

Stay Off Booze Recovery Is Everything To You

*****

SOLUTIONS

Saving Our Lives Using The Inventory Of Needed
Steps

*****

SPONSOR

Sober Person Offering Newcomers Suggestions On
Recovery

*****

STAR

Start Talking About Recovery

*****

STEPS

Solutions To Every Problem in Sobriety
Solutions To Every Problem, Sober
*****

STOP

Sicker Than Other People
*****

TIME

Things I Must Earn
This I Must Earn
This I Must Experience
*****

TRUST

Try Relying Upon The Steps
*****

WASP

Worry Anger Self Pity
*****

WISDOM

When In Self, Discover Our Motives
*****

WORK

What Our Recovery Knows…
*****

WORRY

Wrong Or Right Remain Yourself
*****

WILLING

When I Live Life, I Need God
*****

YET

You're Eligible Too
   You'll End Up There
*****

More Acronyms:

More Acronyms:

Little Quotes From Big Names

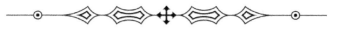

The mentality and behavior of drug addicts and alcoholics is wholly irrational until you understand that they are completely powerless over their addiction and unless they have structured help, they have no hope

— Russel Brand

Hardships often prepare ordinary people for an extraordinary destiny.

— C.S. Lewis

Today you are You, that is truer than true. There is no one alive who is Youer than You.

— Dr. Seuss

I can't change the direction of the wind, but I can adjust my sails to always reach my destination."

— Jimmy Dean

What the caterpillar calls
the end of the world, the
master calls a butterfly.
— Richard Bach

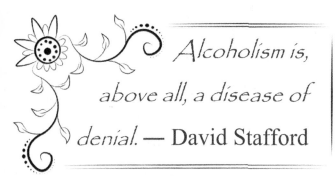

Alcoholism is,
above all, a disease of
denial. — David Stafford

Even the darkest night will
end and the sun will rise.
— Victor Hugo

As one goes through life,
one learns that if you
don't paddle your own
canoe, you don't move.
— Katharine Hepburn

The greatest mistake you can
make in life is to continually be
afraid you will make one.
— Elbert Hubbard

Whether you think you
can or you think you can't,
either way, you're right.
— Henry Ford

You can come out of the
furnace of trouble two ways:
if you let it consume you,
you come out a cinder; but
there is a kind of metal which
refuses to be consumed,
and comes out a star.

— Jean Church

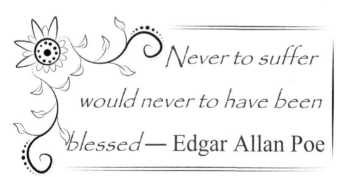

Never to suffer
would never to have been
blessed— Edgar Allan Poe

Rock bottom became the solid foundation on which I rebuilt my life
— JK Rowlings

You don't have to see the whole staircase. Just take the first step
— Martin Luther King

Recovery is an acceptance that your life is in shambles and you have to change.
— Jamie Lea Curtis

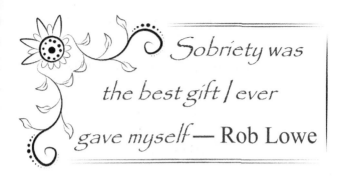

Sobriety was the best gift I ever gave myself — Rob Lowe

We may think there is willpower involved, but more likely ... change is due to want power. Wanting the new addiction more than the old one. Wanting the new me in preference to the person I am now.

— George Sheehan

Sometimes you can only
find Heaven by slowly
backing away from Hell.
— Carrie Fisher

The most common way people
give up their power is by
thinking they don't have any."
— Alice Walker

Experience is not what
happens to you, it is what you
do with what happens to you.
— Aldous Huxley

I realized that I only had two choices: I was either going to die or I was going to live, and which one did I want to do? And then I said those words, 'I'll get help,' or, 'I need help. I'll get help.' And my life turned around. Ridiculous for a human being to take 16 years to say, 'I need help.

— Elton John

I have learned over the years that when one's mind is made up, this diminishes fear.

— Rosa Parks

What lies behind us and what lies before us are tiny matters compared to what lies within us.

— Ralph Waldo Emerson

We can't solve problems by using the same kind of thinking we used when we created them.

— Albert Einstein

I went to hell and back, but I wouldn't have it any other way. Then I wouldn't be in the position I'm in, happy about life and comfortable in my skin.

— Drew Barrymore

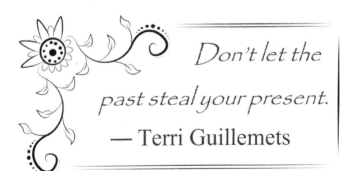

Don't let the past steal your present.

— Terri Guillemets

In the end, some of your greatest pains become your greatest strengths.

— Drew Barrymore

Success is the sum of small efforts, repeated day in and day out.

— Robert Collier

Our greatest glory is not in never failing, but in rising up every time we fail.

— Ralph Waldo Emerson

If things go wrong, don't go with them.
— Roger Babson

Getting sober was one of the three pivotal events in my life, along with becoming an actor and having a child. Of the three, finding my sobriety was the hardest."

— Robert Downey Jr.

Recovery is taking all twelve steps...over and over and over and over...

— Toni Sorenson

Courage isn't having the strength to go on – it's going on when you don't have strength.

— Napoleon Bonaparte

Our wounds are often the openings into the best and most beautiful part of us.

— David Richo

I've been the lead in movies, on television shows and nominated for Emmy. But the best thing I can say about me is that people who can't stop drinking come up to me and say, 'Can you help me?' And I can say, "Yes"

— Matthew Perry

Recovery is hard. Regret is harder.

— Brittany Burgunder

F-E-A-R has two meanings:
"Forget Everything And Run"
or "Face Everything And
Rise." The choice is yours.
— Zig Ziglar

Sometimes when in a dark
place you think you've
been buried, when actually
you've been planted.
— Christine Caine

The way to get started is to
quit talking and begin doing.
— Walt Disney

My identity shifted when I got into recovery. That's who I am now, and it actually gives me greater pleasure to have that identity than to be a musician or anything else, because it keeps me in a manageable size.

— Eric Clapton

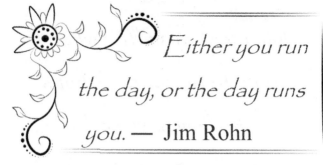

Either you run the day, or the day runs you. — Jim Rohn

Once I was clear-headed, and I hadn't been clear-headed in so long, I was like, I can never go back. And I'm still thankful.
— Travis Barke

Sometimes you've just got to give yourself what you wish someone else would give you.
— Dr. Phil

It's not the load that breaks you down, it's the way you carry it.
— Lou Holtz

Change the way you look at things and the things you look at change.
— Wayne W. Dyer

You may have a fresh start any moment you choose, for this thing we call 'failure' is not the falling down, but the staying down.

— Mary Pickford

Be yourself; everyone else is already taken. — Oscar Wild

Every experience in your life is being orchestrated to teach you something you need to know to move forward."

— Brian Tracy

All the suffering, stress, and addiction comes from not realizing you already are what you are looking for.

— Jon Kabat-Zinn

You must do the things you think you cannot do. — Eleanor Roosevelt

One day you will tell your story of how you overcame what you went though and it will be someone else's survival guide.
— Brene Brown

If you hear a voice within
you say 'you cannot paint,'
then by all means paint and
that voice will be silenced.
— Vincent Van Gogh

Obstacles are those
frightening things that
become visible when we take
our eyes off our goals.
— Henry Ford

The only thing standing
between you and your goal
is the bullshit story you
keep telling yourself as to
why you can't achieve it.
— Jordan Belfort

It always seems
impossible until it's done.
— Nelson Mandela

Have patience with all things, but chiefly have patience with yourself. Do not lose courage in considering your own imperfections, but instantly set about remedying them – every day, begin the task anew.

— Saint Francis de Sales

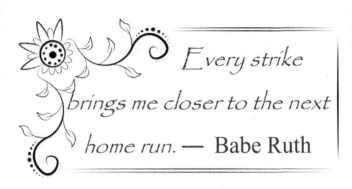

Every strike brings me closer to the next home run. — **Babe Ruth**

You have brains in your head.

You have feet in your shoes.

You can steer yourself any

direction you choose.

— **Dr. Seuss**

Sometimes the smallest step in the right direction ends up being the biggest step of your life. Tiptoe if you must, but take the step.

— Naeem Callaway

Amazing how we can light tomorrow with today.

— Elizabeth Barrett Browning

Far East Wisdom

*When you think
everything is someone else
fault, you will suffer a lot.
When you realize that
everything springs only
from yourself, you will
learn both peace and joy.*

— Dalai Lama

Those who are awake, live in a state of constant amazement.

— Buddha

Do not let the behavior of others destroy your inner peace.

— Dalai Lama

Change your thoughts, change your life."

— Lao Tzu

The journey of a thousand miles begins with a single step.

— Lao Tzu

Our sorrows and wounds
are healed only when we
touch them with compassion.

— Buddha

When I let go of what I am,
I become what I might be.

— Lao Tzu

All that we are, is the result
of what we have thought.
The mind is everything.
What we think, we become.

— Buddha

Zen Proverbs

The diamond cannot be polished without friction, nor the person perfected without trials.

Patience and the mulberry leaf become a silk gown.

The man who moved the mountain was the one who began carrying away the smallest stones.

The best time to plant a tree was 20 years ago. The second best time is now.

Happiness is where we find it, but rarely where we seek it.

It is better to take many small steps in the right direction than to make a great leap forward only to stumble backward

If you want happiness for an hour, take a nap. If you want happiness for a day, go fishing. If you want happiness for a year, inherit a fortune. If you want happiness for a lifetime, help somebody.

A wise man adapts himself to circumstances, as water shapes itself to the vessel that contains it.

Control your emotions or
they will control you.

With true friends, even
water drunk together is
sweet enough.

The temptation to give up is
strongest just before victory.

Let go, or be dragged.

Either don't begin or, having
begun, don't give up.

It is easy to get a thousand
prescriptions but hard to
get one single remedy.

First the man takes a drink,
then the drink takes a drink,
then the drink takes a man.

A strong man overcomes
an obstacle, a wise man
goes the whole way

Just when the caterpillar
thought the world was
over, it became a butterfly

Obstacles don't block the path;
they are the path.

If we are facing in the right
direction, all we have to do
is keep on walking.

*Only when you can be
extremely pliable and soft
can you be extremely hard
and strong.*

Adapt the remedy
to the disease.

More Quotes:

More Quotes:

More Quotes:

More Quotes:

Reasons to Laugh

Defects are like accessories,

I lose one and find another.

THE LIST OF IDEOLOGY SHIT

TAOISM: *Shit happens.*

CONFUCIANISM: *Confucius say "Shit happens."*

BUDDHISM: *Shit happens, but not really.*

HINDUISM: *This shit has happened before.*

ISLAM: *If shit happens, it is the will of Allah.*

CATHOLICISM: *If shit happens, you deserve it.*

LUTHERAN: *If shit happens, don't talk about it.*

PRESBYTERIAN: *This shit was bound to happen.*

BAPTIST: *When shit happens, everybody will go to Hell except us.*

EPISCOPALIAN: *It's not so bad if shit happens, as long as you serve the right wine with it.*

METHODIST: *It's not so bad if shit happens, as long as you serve grape juice with it.*

UNITARIAN: *Come let us reason together about this shit.*

SEVENTH DAY ADVENTISM: *No shit shall happen on Saturday.*

JEHOVAH'S WITNESS: *[KNOCK KNOCK] Shit happens*.

JUDAISM: *Why does this shit always happen to us?*

SCIENTOLOGY: *If shit happens, see Dianetics, p.157*

Rastafarianism: *Smoke that shit!*

SATANISM: *sneppaH tihS*

AGNOSTICISM: *Maybe shit happened, maybe not.*

ATHEISM: *I can't believe this shit.*

NIHILISM: *No shit.*

AA: *Accept that shit happens-- One Day At A Time!*

The truth will set you free, but for an alcoholic, it will first piss us off.

A woman goes to an AA meeting, introduces herself, "I've been through three relationships now and I just can't handle it anymore. My pussy is killing me."

Someone interrupts and asks, "What does this have to do with your alcohol problem?"

"Alcohol? I can't seem to give up the hard lickers!"

The traditions help us from

committing homicide.

The steps help us from

committing suicide;

A sponsor and his sponsee are deserted on an island. They come upon a bottle.

They rub it and a genie appears and says they each get one wish – whatever they want.

The sponsor says, "I wish I were back with my homegroup."
POOF! He disappears.

The sponsee paces nervously around, indecisive, anxious, nervous... Should I ask for money? A woman? A nice boat?

Finally in exasperation he cries out, "I wish my sponsor was here!" POOF!

After the AA meeting,
the ghost finally admitted it.
He has a boos problem.

The doctor said, "I can't find a cause for your illness. Frankly, I think it's due to drinking."

The patient replies, "Then I'll come back when you're sober."

Newcomer: "How do I know how many meetings I should attend each week?"

Old-timer: "Gradually cut back until you drink. Then you'll know."

An alcoholic, a meth user and a prostitute are all in one car. Who's driving?

The Police

The Devil walks into a crowded bar. Within seconds the bar emptied with people running out screaming all over the place, all except for one old timer sat at the bar sipping an orange juice.

The Devil wanders across to the old timer and says "Do you know who I am?" The old timer took another sip of his orange juice and answered "Yep."

The Devil stared at the old timer and asked "Well aren't you afraid of me?"

The old timer looked the Devil up and down for a minute and shrugs "I married your sister 40 years ago, why the hell should I be afraid of you?"

Family knows how to push your buttons because they installed them.

An AA seemed pretty glum when she got home. So her husband asks, "what's wrong?"

"I just learned that I need to stay away from people that trigger my drinking."

"Oh, I'm so sorry dear. It must be sad to have to stay away from people you care about."

"Oh, yes. And what's worse is that I'll have to pay all my own bills after the divorce!".

Good things come to those who...

go out and fucking seize it!

As a newcomer is talking to an old-timer, the who has a heart attack. As he slides down to the floor, the newcomer follows him down still talking about himself.

As the old-timer is laying there gasping and saying "Call 911", the newcomer says "Ok, in just a moment but first, what do you think I should do about this situation I'm in?"

AA is like an adjustable wrench.
It fits every nut.

A man in a hot air balloon realized he was lost. He saw a person on the ground and yelled to him, "Can you help me? I don't know where I am." The man replied, "Sure. You are in a hot air balloon hovering 30 feet above the ground...between 40- and 41-degrees North latitude and between 59- and 60-degrees West longitude."

"Wow, you must be an AA sponsor", said the man in the balloon. "I am", said the man, "but what gave me away?"

"Well," answered the balloonist, "everything you told me is technically right but I am still lost. Frankly you're not much help at all and you might even have delayed my trip."

"You must be an AA sponsee", replied the man. The man in the balloon was amazed and said, "I am, but how did you know?"

The man on the ground said, "Well, you don't know where you are or where you're going. You have risen to where you are due to a lot of hot air. You are expecting other people to solve your problems and the fact is that you are in exactly the same position you were in before we met, but somehow now IT'S MY FAULT"!

AA is the biggest 'Lost and Found' department in the world.

An old wino was sitting at a table waiting for meeting time. In comes a young kid with eyes wide opened with hair standing straight up and dyed many different colors, red, orange, green, blue etc.

The kid looked at the wino and the wino looked at hard at him.

He quickly turned away but felt the cold eyes of the wino staring holes thru the back of his head. He glanced back and saw the wino still staring. Again, he turned away. Finally, the young kid couldn't take it anymore. He jumped up and screamed at the old wino, "dang it old man, haven't you ever got wasted and done sometime weird?"

"Sure!" the wino quietly proclaimed, "I got drunk and made love with a parrot once. I thought you must be my son!"

I was so sick I couldn't have made out in a woman's prison with a pocket full of pardons.

The other day, my friends asked me to go out to a bar with them, so I gave them a list of things I'm going to need to prevent relapse.
1. New friends

If you can't laugh at yourself, can I?

A man and his wife were awoken at 3:00 am by a loud pounding on the door. The man gets up and goes to the door where a drunken stranger, standing in the pouring rain, is asking for a push.

"No way," says the husband, "it is 3:00 am!" and slammed the door.

When he tells his wife, she responds with, "You should be ashamed. Don't you remember about three months ago when we broke down, and those two guys helped us? I think you should help the guy!"

So, the man gets dressed and goes out in the pouring rain.

He calls into the dark, "Hello, are you still there?"

"Yes," he hears.

"Do you still need a push?" asks the husband.

"Yes, please!" comes the reply from the dark.

"Where are you?" asks the husband.

"Over here on the swing," replied the drunk

I called AA by mistake...
Those drunks can't change a
tire for shit!

If you like everyone in AA, you haven't been to enough meetings.

I'm sorry, are the noises in my
head bothering you?

I don't care who you are or what you've done. Anyone who chooses recovery over a life of addiction is a fucking Soldier!

I was always the black sheep.
Then I started going to meetings
and found the rest of my herd.

My only regret in finding my sobriety so early in my life is that I didn't have enough time to tell more people to fuck-off!

Now that I'm a reformed alcoholic I realize I'm still the same asshole but with fewer dents in my car. - Robin Williams

The next time something goes wrong in your life, just yell, "PLOT TWIST!" and move on.

THE 12 FUCKING STEPS:

Step 1. I'm fucked up

Step 2. There might be way out of this fucking mess?

Step 3. Decided to level the fuck up

Step 4. Took a good hard look at how fucked up I am

Step 5. Tell someone all the fucked-up shit I did

Step 6. Prepare to stop being such a fuck up

Step 7. Try to stop acting so fucked up

Step 8. Make a list of everyone I fucked over

Step 9. Swallow my fucking pride & tell them how I fucked up except when it would fuck them up more

Step 10. Keep an eye on my fucked-up thinking and behavior

Step 11. Chill the fuck out sometimes

Step 12. Help the next fucker who walks in the door

An Alcoholic walks into a bar and orders three pints of Guinness.

The bartender brings him the three pints and the man proceeds to alternately sip one, then the other, then the third until they're gone, then orders three more.

The bartender says, "Sir, you don't have to order three at a time. I can keep an eye out and when you get low, I'll bring you a fresh cold one."

The Alcoholic thanks the bartender and says, "That's not why I order three at a time. You see, I have one brother is in Australia and one in the States. We made a vow that every Saturday night we'd still drink together. So right now, my brothers have three pints of Guinness too, so we're drinking together.

The bartender thought that was a wonderful tradition.

Every week the man came in and ordered three beers. Then one week he came in and only ordered two.

The bartender said to him, "I know what your tradition is, and I'd just like to say that I'm sorry you lost one of your brothers."

The Alcoholic said, "Oh, my brothers are fine. I just quit drinking."

Dear alcohol, we had a deal that you would make me prettier, funnier, and smarter. I saw the video... we need to talk.

A treatment center is where you go and pay $15,000 to find out that A. A. meetings are free.

I drank so much that my blood type is now AA.

Newcomer: "Excuse me, can you tell me how to get to AA?"
Old-timer: "Sure! First, go straight to hell, then make a U-turn."

I obsessively pursue feeling good... no matter how bad it makes me feel.

The newcomer said to his sponsor, "Well, that's enough about me now, let's talk about you. What do you think about me?"

An old-timer was asked,
"What are the 12 Steps?"
He responds, "Job training
to sponsor people."

A female newcomer asked her sponsor what the Big Book advises about sex. The Sponsor told her to read page 69 which is where the book discusses the sex part of the 4th Step Inventory.

When she got home, she eagerly turned to page 96 (transposing the page number.) Here's what she read on page 96:

Do not be discouraged if your prospect does not respond at once. Search out another alcoholic and try again. You are sure to find someone desperate enough to accept with eagerness what you offer.

Newcomer: "How long do I
have to go to meetings?"
Old-timer: "Until you die of
something else."

Paddy was getting on his wife's nerves. She scolded, "Do something! Get out of here! Take the dog for a walk!"

Paddy was a little dense, but he was no fool, he took the dog for a walk to the pub.

Paddy tied the dog and entered the pub for a 'few'. More dogs gathered around outside and trouble started.

After a while a policeman entered and inquired, " Who has a dog tied outside?"

Paddy replied, "That is my dog." The cop said, "Sir did you know that your dog is in heat?"

Paddy was a little slow and he answered, "In Heat? No, no, no, I tied her in the shade!"

The cop rolled his eyes and said, "Sir you don't understand. Your dog want's bred."

"Bread?" replied Paddy, "I just fed her before we came here!"

Exasperated the cop leaned in close to Paddy and whispered, "Your dog wants to have sex!"

Paddy stepped back and looked the cop in the eye as he thought about it a moment. Then he smiled and winked at the cop and said, "OK then! Go ahead! I always wanted a police dog!"

Sobriety is the leading cause of relapse.

God grant me a vacation to make bearable what I cannot change, a friend to make it funny, and the wisdom to never get my panties in a bunch because it doesn't solve anything and makes me walk funny.

An alcoholic without a sponsor is like Dracula being in charge of the blood bank.

I've got 99 problems and 96 of them are completely made-up scenarios in my head that I'm stressing about for absolutely no logical reason.

I never make the same mistake twice. I make it seven or eight times. You know. Just to be sure.

The difference between a problem drinker and an Alcoholic is that:

A) When the alcohol is taken away from the problem drinker, the problem goes away.

B) When the alcohol is taken away from the Alcoholic, the problem begins.

TWELVE THINGS IN A NEWCOMER'S LIFE:

12. Steps to work
11. Friends still fuming
10. New found triggers
9. New phone numbers
8. Friends to dump
7. Meetings to attend
6. Places to avoid
5. Bottles of water
4. Phone calls
3. Pots of coffee
2. Books to read
1. Day at a time!

This is a 'One Day at a Time' program. If you're clean and sober today, you are tied for first place in AA.

Why do they call the back row at an AA meeting the "shoe department"?

That's where you can find the slippers and loafers!

What's the difference between a heavy drinker and an alcoholic?

When a heavy drinker gets a DUI he says "ugh, I shouldn't have had that last shot."

When an alcoholic gets a DUI he says "ugh, I should have taken a different street home."

Recovery brought my head outta my ass. Just for today, I no longer live in a world of shit!

Newcomer: "My conscience finally brought me to the Program."

Old-timer: "How so?"

Newcomer: " I kept seeing this eyeball staring at me from the bottom of the glass! I'm sure it was my conscience."

Old-timer: "Probably just an olive. But never mind---whatever works!"

ASKHOLE: Someone constantly asking for your advice then always doing the opposite.

A man fell off a cliff. He was able to grab ahold of a small tree. As he dangled there, with the abyss below, he called out "Is there anyone up there?"

A booming voice answers "Yes, it is I. God."

Terrified, the man begs God to help. God says "Okay, just let go."

The man thinks it over, then yells "Is there anyone else up there?"

Statistics show that 10 out of 10 people die.
So stop take life so fucking seriously!

They say don't burn bridges because you might need to cross them later.

I say, I don't mind swimming if the bridge was already fucked up to begin with.

An AA meeting is like an

orgy...when it's over you feel better,

but you're not sure who to thank.

So, they say I don't need meetings to stay sober.

Well, I don't need shoes to walk down a gravel road either but it sure fucking helps!

Alcoholics are insane. Not because we do the same thing over and over and expect different results. But because we repeatedly do things knowing full well what the shitty outcome will be.

It's funny when people try to manipulate, hustle, or lie, to us now. Like, "Bitch, you can't fool me. I'm an addict. I wrote the book on that shit!"

I've never done anything in moderation

— except maybe these steps.

Grant me the serenity to accept stupid people the way they are, courage to maintain self-control,
And wisdom to know if I act on it, I'll go to jail.

The good news is that you get your emotions back! The bad news is that you get your emotions back!

More funny shit:

More funny shit:

More funny shit:

More funny shit:

More funny shit:

More From Imaginate

THE BOLD & BRAVE:

The Smoker's Way To Quit: (Trigger Tracker)
Five Minute Guided Trigger Tracker
5 Minute Guided Trigger Tracker With Journal
AA Powerful 12 Step Workbook
AA 12 step workbook: Twelve Steps Journal
The First 90 Days: 12 Step Workbook
Fourth Step Workbook: AA Journal For Recovery
Making Our 4-Column Grudge List: Step 4 Journal
Swapping Character Defects For Character Assets
The Next Six Months: 10th Step Journal
10th Step Inventory Journal
My 10th Step Inventory Journal

A BELIEVER'S TOOLBOX:

A Chronological Bible Reading Plan & Journal
4-Month Bible Study Planner & Journal
Bible Study Journal: Drawing Closer To God
Gratitude Journal With Quotes From The Bible
200 Page Notebook With Quotes From The Bible
Undated Planner & Bible Study Journal
2023 Planner & Bible Study Journal

SUCCESS IS PLANNED ~ PLANNERS

JOURNALS FROM IMAGINATE

COMPOSITION NOTEBOOKS

Made in the USA
Middletown, DE
07 December 2024